Original title:
The Meaning of Life According to the Universe

Copyright © 2025 Creative Arts Management OÜ
All rights reserved.

Author: Mariana Leclair
ISBN HARDBACK: 978-1-80566-132-0
ISBN PAPERBACK: 978-1-80566-427-7

Twilight Dialogues with the Infinite

In the cosmos vast and wide,
Stars giggle at our pride.
Planets spin, and suns do wink,
While we ponder, breathe, and drink.

Galaxies swirl like cotton candy,
As black holes grin, a bit dandy.
Meteor showers throw confetti,
'The universe parties, aren't we ready?'

Comets race, with tails aglow,
While we chase time, moving slow.
But who knows, in this grand jest,
If the moon just needs a rest?

So raise a glass to our grand quest,
As life unfolds, we jest and jest.
Among the stars, we'll gamble, groove,
Finding joy in all that we move!

Mysteries in the Fabric of Space

In the cosmic quilt, a cat might nap,
Planets giggle, caught in a trap.
Stars wiggle and dance, a celestial show,
While black holes sigh, 'Where did they go?'

Wormholes whisper secrets, silly but bold,
Time's like a jigsaw, a puzzle to unfold.
Aliens ponder over veggie fries,
Are we the punchline in their weird skies?

The Pulse of Existence

Heartbeat of atoms, thump-thump in sync,
Life's like a drink, might spill with a wink.
Galaxies swirl in a wacky ballet,
Cosmic confusion, what's next in the play?

Comets chuckle as they zip and zoom,
While quasars beam brightly in their own little room.
Is life just a game of hide and seek?
With echoes of laughter from the stars that peek?

Between Light and Dark

Between dark and light, we take a chance,
Photons are doing a crazy dance.
Shadows giggle, casting a tease,
As twilight whispers, "Who needs a breeze?"

In a black hole's belly, secrets reside,
Jokes of the cosmos, it's hard to decide.
Are we just bugs on a galactic rug?
Or chess pieces played by some cosmic thug?

Cosmic Lullabies

Twinkling stars hum a bedtime tune,
While moons juggle cheese, oh what a boon!
Galaxies snore on the edge of a night,
And meteors squeal in a thrilling flight!

Crickets debate over the best space fries,
While planets play poker, oh what a surprise!
Are we all dreams in a giant's head?
Or just bedtime stories the cosmos said?

Cosmic Lullabies of Being

Stars giggle in the night,
As we ponder our quirky plight.
Planets dance in silly tune,
While comets wink at the moon.

Life's a game of cosmic hide,
Where reason takes a bumpy ride.
We ask the void, what's your plan?
And hear it laugh, 'Just be a fan!'

Fragments of Stardust and Time

Rolling rocks and cosmic dust,
In galaxies, we laugh, we trust.
A black hole swallows my last sock,
While quasars tick like a cosmic clock.

Bouncing meteors, what a sight!
Whisper secrets through the night.
Is life a bubble, bright and brief?
Or just a cosmic comic relief?

A Journey through Celestial Questions

Do aliens giggle at our dreams?
Or stare in awe at our ice creams?
We float in space, a clumsy dance,
As Jupiter gives a cosmic glance.

Do stars take selfies with their flare?
And nebulae breathe in the frosty air?
Each question floats like stardust fine,
In this universe, is there a punchline?

Beneath the Canopy of Infinity

Beneath the stars, we sit and muse,
On what's the point—wait, did we snooze?
A cosmic joke, a riddle spun,
With gravity pulling, we just have fun.

Infinity rolls its eyes, so bright,
While we chase dreams like fireflies at night.
Life's a puzzle, with missing pieces,
But laughter's the light that never ceases.

Mapping the Unseen

Stars flicker like laughter, up in the night,
Charting reasons for being, oh what a sight!
Galaxies swirl, with a giggle and spin,
While black holes joke, 'Join us, if you dare within!'

Nebulae puff, like cosmic cotton candy,
Each planet grins, their orbits so dandy.
Comets tail off, with a wink and a tease,
'Catch us if you can, we're not hard to please!'

Reflections from Celestial Waters

Ripples of laughter dance on starlit lakes,
As cosmic puns bubble, the universe quakes.
'Just float and relax,' the moons softly hum,
Life's just a game, so where's all the fuss come?

Meteor showers drop in with flair,
'Take cover!' they shout, 'if you dare!'
Yet everyone chuckles, dodging their fate,
In this cosmic pool, it's never too late!

The Art of Cosmic Serenity

Life's a canvas painted with astrological hues,
Each brushstroke a wink, as if the stars muse.
Saturn's rings spin tales of old and new,
While Venus winks, 'You should try my perfume!'

Galactic paint splatters across endless skies,
As comets play hopscotch, dodging surprise.
So grab your sketchbook, and take a seat,
The universe waits, with joy at your feet!

In Search of Stellar Wisdom

Wise old quasars laugh, lighting up the dark,
Confessing their secrets, just like a lark.
'What's the secret?' whispers a curious star,
'Life's just a joke; here's wishing on a czar!'

Asteroids wander, with no set course,
As if life's a road trip, fueled by pure force.
Each collision a laugh, every bump a grin,
In this vast expanse, we all share the spin!

Fragments of Stardust Memories

In the cosmic dance of whims,
We twirl like dust on solar winds.
Each twinkle holds a secret grin,
A giggle from where we begin.

Stars giggle as we make our plans,
While galaxies throw cosmic jams.
Planets spin, such playful tricks,
With comet tails and cosmic kicks.

Black holes laugh at our small fears,
While asteroids shed joyful tears.
In vastness, there's a silly play,
As stardust dreams, hip-hip-hooray!

The Great Cosmic Tapestry

Woven threads of laughter bright,
Galactic looms spin day and night.
Each quasar hums a quirky tune,
While moons play hopscotch 'neath the moon.

Nebulas burst with vibrant paint,
In cosmic art that won't grow faint.
A tapestry of funny sights,
Where gravity knots our silly flights.

The universe winks in delight,
As comets streak across the night.
From supernovas to black clads,
Life's a joke that nobody understands!

Navigating the Quantum Sea

Sailing on a wave of chance,
Quantum bubbles start to dance.
With particles in silly socks,
We surf through time, avoiding clocks.

Fuzzy logic makes us chuckle,
As neutrinos give a gentle shuffle.
Entangled hearts on a wave's crest,
In this ocean, we find our jest.

Every thought's a playful spark,
In the dark, we chase a lark.
Navigating with a wink and smile,
Quantum tides, let's stay awhile!

Seasons of the Infinite Spiral

Springtime brings a cosmic tease,
Starflowers bloom with playful ease.
In summer's heat, the suns unite,
Sizzling jokes that feel just right.

Autumn leaves in quirky spins,
As winter wraps in snowy grins.
Galactic seasons come and go,
They dance in circles, putting on a show.

Each spiral arm a comic line,
Inherent jest in each design.
We laugh as time loops back and forth,
In this spiral, we find our worth!

Ripples across the Fabric of Being

In a cosmic pool, a splash we make,
Giggling stars at the mess we shake.
Planets dance in their silly shoes,
As comets giggle, spreading the news.

Life's a riddle wrapped in a pun,
Like a dark horse under a bright sun.
Infinity's joke, we're part of the jest,
Finding our way—a quirky quest.

Stargazers' Delights

Look up at night, what do we see?
A giant disco ball, wild and free!
Planets twirling in cosmic delight,
While aliens chuckle at our plight.

With telescopes aimed at the woozy sky,
We search for answers with an awkward sigh.
But maybe they're laughing, up there, so bright,
At earthlings chasing dreams, day and night.

Language of the Eternal Cosmos

Stars chatter softly in a cosmic choir,
Oh, how they laugh at our human desire!
Galaxies spin their tales of sheer fun,
While meteors race—oh, they can run!

Time's a joker, pulling our leg,
With each tick-tock, we dance and beg.
The universe grins, saying, 'Be bold!'
Find joy in the chaos, let life unfold!

Whispered Secrets of Ancient Stars

Ancient stars whisper, 'Hey, don't you fret!'
Life's but a game you can't fully threat.
Catch a wish on a shooting star,
Just make sure you don't lose your car!

Humans ponder, seeking the clue,
While the cosmos giggles, 'We're watching you!'
So raise your glass to the nebulae vast,
We're but a blip, but oh, what a blast!

Celestial Reflections

Planets spin with joy, so spry,
Stars wink down like they're a bit shy.
Galaxies swirling in a cosmic ballet,
Who knew space could be so cliché?

Black holes suck doubts into their depth,
Supernovae burst like a surprise step.
The comets trail tails, quite a sight,
Cosmic humor woven through the night.

Beneath the Veil of Stars

Under a blanket of cosmic dust,
We all ask why—it's a must!
Asteroids bump with a playful cheer,
Who knew the cosmos had such flair?

Wormholes open like a cosmic door,
Spaghetti theories, we all explore.
Life's quirks dance like asteroids pitter-pat,
Maybe in space, there's a great big cat!

Echoes of Creation

In the beginning, there was a big bang,
Maybe it was just a universe slang.
Stars whisper secrets in twinkling light,
While meteors tease with a playful fright.

Atoms giggle in a cosmic soup,
Quarks and leptons form a merry troupe.
Like a cosmic joke, we're all in on it,
The universe chuckles, not giving a split!

The Dance of Cosmic Forces

Gravity waltzes with a forceful leap,
While planets jive and comets peep.
Neutrons and protons do the cha-cha,
Even light beams in a quirky maraca.

Electromagnetic fields sway in glee,
As quarks twirl like they're at a jamboree.
The universe's dance is one wild spree,
So grab your partner and join in with me!

Through the Eyes of an Ancient Star

Twinkle, twinkle, little light,
Are you really out of sight?
Counting planets, what a game,
Always playing cosmic fame.

I blink at Earth, they wave back,
Wonders bright, but time they lack.
Is that a comet? Oh, how fun!
Time flies fast; I'm just a pun.

Life's a dance around the sun,
Chasing shadows, oh what fun!
Why so serious, eight or nine?
Let's just laugh and drink some wine.

When black holes sigh and stars collapse,
I giggle loud, no need for maps.
We're all stardust, make no fuss,
In laughter's glow, we find our trust.

The Heartbeat of All That Is

In the void, a heartbeat thrums,
Pulsing fast, you hear the drums?
Galaxies take turns to sway,
Like cosmic kids in games we play.

Planets spinning, what a sight,
Wobbling on their axis right.
"Is that a noodle?" comets jest,
Floating past, they're off to fest.

Laughter echoing through the dark,
Dusty trails of a shooting spark.
Life's just a cosmic joke, you see,
And all the stars are laughing free.

So take a step on milky lanes,
Dance with glee and shake those chains.
In the grand scheme, what's a day?
Not much at all - let's laugh and sway!

Cosmic Mirrors of Thought

Reflections in the cosmic sea,
Who's that star? Is it just me?
I wink from Mars, it winks back,
Join my party, don't lose track.

Thoughts collide like meteorite,
Sparking joy, what pure delight!
"Gravity's a pain!" one shouts,
But laughter's what it's all about.

Through the void, our giggles race,
In this space, we find our place.
Planets playing peek-a-boo,
Waving hands, it's a grand view!

So let's engage in cosmic fun,
Life's short, so let's run and run.
In the mirrors where we stand,
We're all quirky, never bland.

Echoing Through the Eons

Across the eons, echoes chime,
Tickling stars through space and time.
"Is that a nebula I see?"
"Of course, but laugh, don't disagree!"

Bouncing jokes from star to star,
Cosmic giggles travel far.
"I've seen a planet made of cheese,"
"Eat the moon? Oh yes, please!"

Whispers of the past collide,
In this void, we all can hide.
Can you hear the cosmic song?
Join the dance and sing along!

As comets blaze and meteors fall,
Laughing softly, we share it all.
Life's a riddle wrapped in jest,
A universe that loves to test.

Shifting Sands of Time

Time's a prankster with a grin,
It shifts the sands, lets chaos win.
Tick-tock, tick-tock, a dance so sly,
You blink, it's gone, oh my, oh my.

We chase our dreams like cats on yarn,
But life's a joke, not meant to harm.
A twist, a turn, a slight detour,
In search of gold, we find a boar!

So fret not, folks, don't be so grim,
Just laugh it off when times get slim.
For every hour that spins away,
Brings chocolate cake and bright bouquet.

In this vast, wild cosmic play,
Let's spin and tumble, laugh all day.
With every star that winks at night,
We find our joy, our silly light.

The Universe's Gentle Whisper

Behind every star a secret's hid,
The universe chuckles, a cheeky kid.
It whispers softly, 'What's your goal?'
But then shouts loud, 'Just play your role!'

We run in circles, oh what a race,
Chasing our tails in outer space.
The cosmos giggles at our haste,
Dressing us up in a funny lace.

So here's a riddle from the sky,
Why is a comet so very shy?
Because it streaks with a gleeful flair,
Then hides as if nobody's there!

In life's grand script of jest and rhyme,
Each plot twist spills a goofy crime.
Embrace the quirks of this vast design,
The universe laughs; so should we, divine.

Understanding through Distant Galaxies

Across the void, the stars inflect,
Sending giggles we can detect.
Oh little Earth, so blissfully wild,
Lost in your dreams, like a child.

Galaxies twirl in a cosmic dance,
While we sit here, caught in a trance.
They wink and nod, so far away,
And share their tales of new cliché.

Comets crashing, nebulae spun,
In the vast dark, we're all just fun.
With telescopes aimed, we hope to find,
A joke tucked neatly in space and time.

So let's toast to mishaps, joys, and fears,
As laughter echoes through the years.
In every quasar's glimmer and gleam,
Is a ticklish tickle, a cosmic dream.

A Cosmic Mosaic of Meaning

In this mural of space, a funny sight,
Planets giggle and stars ignite.
Each patch of black, each splotch of light,
Creates a puzzle both bold and bright.

Galaxies clash like kids at play,
Making mischief in their own way.
A sprinkle of humor in every star,
We laugh and wander, life's bizarre.

So don't get lost in the serious quest,
For meaning's nestled in jest, not rest.
With every supernova's echoing laugh,
We find our way on this silly path.

The universe crafts with whimsical flair,
In this grand design, oh, who would care?
For the fun we share is life's best gift,
A cosmic chuckle; let your spirit lift!

Celestial Conversations with the Void

Stars chat with the black, quite bold,
A cosmic joke that's often told.
Planets spin in a silly dance,
While asteroids prank like they've got a chance.

Galaxies swirl with a wink and grin,
Shooting stars know where to begin.
Quasars laugh like it's all a game,
While dark matter hides in cosmic fame.

Threads of Time in the Cosmic Weave

Time's a fabric, a wobbly thread,
Stitching moments, where dreams are fed.
Wormholes poke fun at plans we make,
Laughs echo loud in the great bellyache.

Gravity trips on its way to the sun,
Twirling through space, just having fun.
Black holes giggle, 'come here, take a peek!'
But they tend to munch on the cheeky and weak.

Eclipses of Understanding

The moon covers the sun, a playful tease,
While planets giggle in cosmic breeze.
Life's just a shadow, a wink in time,
A dance that's silly, though wrapped in rhyme.

Comets graze by with ridiculous tails,
Leaving behind a trail of tales.
Eclipses nudge us, 'Hey, look over here!'
As if the cosmos holds too much beer.

The Symmetry of Stellar Fate

Stars twinkle and wink, like they're in on a plot,
Planets spin daintily, conceiving their thought.
Life's a riddle wrapped tight in a spin,
As galaxies giggle, 'Oh, where to begin?'

The universe wobbles, a perfect pirouette,
With equations that chuckle, and puzzles unmet.
Cosmic chaos is quite the thrill,
For those who dance on the universe's grill.

The Universe's Silent Lullaby

Stars are winking, eyes so bright,
They giggle softly, deep in the night.
Planets spin in their quirky dance,
While comets laugh, given half a chance.

Galaxies swirl, a cosmic joke,
Black holes chuckle, they'll never choke.
Time ticks on, with a wink and a grin,
In this grand scheme, let the silliness begin!

Eternal Patterns in Celestial Light

Patterns emerge, like dots on a map,
While aliens stare, and say, "What a trap!"
Constellations gossip, forming their cliques,
As nebulas giggle with colorful tricks.

Every dark void holds a joke or two,
With quarks and leptons dancing, woohoo!
Life's a puzzle, a cosmic game,
Just hope your pieces stay somewhat the same!

An Odyssey Through Cosmic Wonders

Rockets zooming, what a wild ride,
Asteroids shout, "Come join the side!"
Meteor showers bring laughter and cheer,
As space dust whispers, "We're all pioneers!"

Planets whisper secrets in their own tongues,
While moons play hopscotch, with joyful youngs.
It's a universe big, but it's quite a laugh,
Where even black holes enjoy a good gaffe!

Reflections on an Infinite Canvas

The cosmos paints with colors so rare,
While supernovas do their hair!
Each star reflects, a giggle or two,
Making wishes on dreams that come true.

Painting those thoughts with asteroids' flair,
With light-speed humor blasting through air.
In this infinite mix of giggles and sighs,
Life's one big laugh under endless skies!

The Great Infinite Dialogue

In a bar made of stardust, stars sip on gin,
 Galaxies laugh over cosmic chagrin.
'Is sushi from Saturn better than cheese?'
'Try Jupitarian tacos, they aim to please!'

Black holes whisper secrets, no one can hear,
'What's life like on Earth?' 'A bit insincere!'
'You'd think it's all gold, but it's mostly just dust,'
Yet here we all are, in the universe's rust!

Celestial Dreams and Earthly Laments

Planets spin tales in celestial tones,
While humans complain about their lost phones.
'What's your purpose?' the meteors jest,
'Get some more snacks and just be our guest!'

The sun wears sunglasses, so cool and aloof,
While life on Earth seeks its next great goof.
Stars crowd together, sharing a laugh,
'If we're all stardust, let's make a craft!'

Through the Lens of Time and Space

Time-twisted clocks tick with cosmic delight,
While Earthlings debate if daylight feels bright.
'What's a comet's secret to such a great tail?'
'Just a whole lotta dust and a laugh without fail!'

Nebulae giggle in colors so bold,
'Come watch humans, they're a sight to behold!'
Through lenses of time, they ponder their fate,
'Why not relax? It's a long, winding wait!'

Constellations of Wonder and Sorrow

Constellations wink, what a cheeky bunch,
While Earthlings are busy planning their lunch.
'Is it fate or bad luck that we're stuck in a groove?'
'Just ride out the waves, and keep trying to move!'

Stars in their orbits, a celestial dance,
While we trip over gravity, missing our chance.
In laughter and chaos, the universe beams,
Maybe life's best in twinkling dreams!

Patterns of Light and Shadow

In the sky, a dance takes flight,
Stars are giggling, oh what a sight!
Planets spin in a cosmic race,
While comets play tag, keeping pace.

The sun throws shade, like a sneaky friend,
Whispers of laughter never seem to end.
Jupiter yawns and Saturn wears rings,
Even black holes have a chuckle with swings.

Each twinkle, a wink from afar,
Life's a joke; we're the bizarre.
Galaxies swirl, casting fun vibes,
In this comic void where humor thrives.

So dance with the stars through the night,
Laugh at the shadows, hold on tight.
For each fleeting moment, embrace the giggle,
In the cosmic play, the universe wiggles.

The Language of the Stars

Blinky lights in the velvet sky,
Stars whisper secrets, oh me, oh my!
They giggle in Morse—did you catch the news?
A supernova came to the interstellar blues!

They chat through the night, light-years apart,
Filling dark voids with laughter, that's art!
Constellations connect like a cosmic joke,
Even black holes chew stars like a smoke!

Meteor showers rain down surprise,
Wishing on bright dots that dance in the skies.
Life's a pun in a galaxy grand,
And stars are the jesters, oh isn't it grand?

So tune into winks and celestial cheers,
For the universe giggles across the spheres.
In a comedy where no one feels blue,
The language of stars speaks just to you!

In Pursuit of the Unknowable

Chasing questions through regions unknown,
Scientists fuss but their minds seem blown!
What is the universe's ultimate quirk?
Is it time or space that likes to smirk?

They ponder and wonder, shaking their heads,
While quasars chuckle, fueling their dreads.
A Planck length tickles curious minds,
In the chase for knowledge, humor unwinds.

Galactic quests, with answers so few,
Bouncing around like a cosmic debut.
Does dark matter giggle at the light?
In pursuit of the unknowable, what a delight!

So laugh in the chase, with theories absurd,
Who needs answers when laughter's the word?
Embrace all the quirks and the cosmic dance,
For in mystery's arms, we find our chance.

Cosmic Joy and Sorrow

In the galaxy's embrace, joy swirls bright,
Yet sadness slips in like a shadowy sprite.
Stars shine in laughter, while planets might pout,
Life's a rollercoaster, there's little doubt!

Nebulae bloom like a cosmic bouquet,
Yet supernovae crash, lighting the way.
In joys and in sorrows, the universe sways,
Winking and basking in glorious rays.

Comets cry, then they sparkle with glee,
As black holes consume what we cannot see.
Life and loss in a stellar ballet,
Dancing together in colorful play.

So toast to the joys and the bittersweet pain,
In the tapestry woven, we're all just a chain.
For in laughter and tears, we find our own song,
In cosmic delight, we all belong!

Time as an Endless River

Time flows like a river, so grand,
You splash in its waters, take a stand,
With fish that insist on doing the cha-cha,
While ducks argue over who's the big kahuna.

Moments drift by like boats made of dreams,
Caught in the currents of cosmic schemes,
Should we paddle faster, or take a long nap?
Oh, life's just a voyage, let's skip the old map!

The clock ticks away with a hiccup or two,
Sipping on coffee, what else can you do?
As time does the tango, I laugh and I spin,
For even the seconds wear goofy grins.

So here we float, in this silly parade,
With time as a river, let's serenade,
Each moment a splash, a stumble, a dive,
In this endless wet party, we thrive and jive.

Interstellar Questions

Out in the cosmos where oddities gleam,
Aliens ponder, is life just a meme?
Do stars get together for cosmic tea?
Or swap silly jokes, like you and me?

Black holes are just vacuum cleaners, right?
Sucking up stardust, out of sheer fright,
And planets debate if they're round or they're square,
While comets run past with a stylish flair.

What's on Jupiter's menu, a storm or a pie?
Will Saturn invite us for rings made of sky?
As we orbit around these absurd little quests,
The universe chuckles, it knows we're its jest.

Life's Quantum Dances

In the realm of particles, they wiggle and sway,
Atoms break-dance in a quirky ballet,
A photon jumps in a dazzling feat,
While electrons giggle, they can't keep the beat.

Superpositions make us feel quite absurd,
Am I here or there? Oh, haven't you heard?
I'll flip a coin, heads or tails, who knows?
Life's just a dance with some quantum JoJo's.

Entangled with laughter, we bounce through the void,
While chaos conspires, yet we're not destroyed,
Every quirk and quip makes the cosmos a stage,
As we twirl to the rhythms of this cosmic age.

So laugh with the atoms, embrace their delight,
In this quantum ballet that lasts through the night,
For life is a party, unpredictable, grand,
Where every twinkle and giggle is perfectly planned.

Threads of Fate Weaved in Starlight

In the loom of the cosmos, we weave with our dreams,
Threads of existence, or so it seems,
Fate's fabric ripples, all tangled and spun,
While we trip on our stitches, making it fun.

Stars sparkle above, like tiny bling bling,
Telling us secrets that they cannot sing,
"Stay in your lane, or cross it with flair,
The universe laughs at our clumsy despair!"

Sewing our patterns with humorous grace,
Each stitch a reminder we're part of this race,
We dance to a rhythm of cosmic ballet,
With giggles and hiccups along the way.

So gather your threads, let's start a new tale,
In this tapestry woven, where folly prevails,
For the cosmos is crafty, with jokes up its sleeve,
And in laughter and chaos, we truly believe.

Whispers of Cosmic Truth

In the vastness, stars do dance,
Planets spin in a cosmic prance.
Black holes snicker, hiding their snacks,
While comets race, with no time to relax.

Galaxies giggle, twirling around,
Echoes of laughter, a playful sound.
Asteroids chuckle, dodging their fate,
While quasars hum a tune that's first-rate.

Nebulas blush in swirling hues,
Confetti of stardust in cosmic news.
Life's a riddle, or maybe a joke,
With the universe grinning—what's up with that poke?

So join the waltz, feel the sunbeam,
Life's a wild ride, a hilarious dream.
In the cosmos, all's well and good,
Beneath the laughter, we all understood.

Stars and Silent Questions

Twinkling lights in the night sky,
Are they just playing? Oh my, oh my!
What's their secret? Do they hold a clue?
Or sip on starlight in a cosmic brew?

Planets tease, spinning on a dime,
Rolling dice as if keeping time.
"Who's the boss?" asks a cheeky moon,
While suns burst forth with a fiery tune.

In this great game, what's the score?
Do meteors know what they're shooting for?
Tiny green aliens giggle above,
For life on Earth is truly a shove.

Yet here we sit, pondering our fate,
Joking with stars, it's never too late.
In this cosmic stage, let's dance and play,
In laughter and wonder, we'll find our way.

Where Time Meets Infinity

Tick-tock goes the cosmic clock,
But time, it seems, is not just a rock.
It bends and stretches, does a funny dive,
Tickling moments to keep them alive.

If days could giggle and seconds could sing,
Would they share jokes about time traveling?
A wink from the past, a nudge from the 'now',
"Hey there, future! Just take a bow!"

Hang on tight, for the ride's quite a blast,
Where moments loop and time flies fast.
In this endless game, there's humor to find,
And thoughts that twist like spaghetti, entwined.

So laugh with the ages, let worries flee,
For in this vast cosmos, we're wild and free.
Time's a partner, so let's take a chance,
In this whimsical waltz, let's join the dance.

The Symphony of Existence

In the grand orchestra of the night,
Stars play notes of sheer delight.
Planets thump in a rhythmic beat,
While black holes hum a tune so sweet.

Comets swoosh like a wild trombone,
Playing solos that set the tone.
Galaxies twirl in an elegant sway,
While nebulas burst in colorful display.

Life's a concerto with laughter and cheer,
Where we all play, from far to near.
Get your instruments, it's time to unite,
In this cosmic jam, everything feels right.

So join in the music, embrace every sound,
For in this symphony, joy can be found.
With every heartbeat, let laughter ring,
In the universe's wild, whimsical swing.

The Universe's Silent Letter

In the cosmic mail, I found a note,
It was written in stars, but hard to quote.
An alien laughed, said, "It's all a game,
Just don't forget to spell my name!"

From Jupiter's rings to Saturn's moans,
I searched for wisdom among the drones.
They told tales of life, and cosmic cheese,
But what to serve at space's teas?

Time bends like a funny worm,
Everyone's dancing with no concern.
"Hey! What's the rush?" a quasar winked,
Life's just a joke, or so I think!

Forget the textbooks and profound thoughts,
The universe giggles, and laughs a lot.
I sent a wish to the Milky Way,
And got a response: "Just dance and sway!"

Galactic Revelations

The stars conspired over cosmic pie,
With apple comets and mint-frosted sky.
In a black hole café, I took a seat,
Where time stood still, but snacks were sweet.

Planets debated what life's about,
Pluto mentioned pizza, some with doubt.
Venus threw in soft, cheesy puns,
While Mars just grumbled and ate his buns.

Asteroids danced in a wobbly line,
While comets made jokes about space and time.
Galactic elders, wise and aloof,
Said, "Life is a riddle, now here's the proof!"

"Toss your worries to the cosmic breeze,
And watch the laughter float with ease.
When in doubt, just spin and twirl,
The universe giggles, give it a whirl!"

Embracing the Void's Embrace

In the forest of nothing, I found a friend,
A shadow of space with no need to pretend.
"Why fret about tomorrow?" said the void,
"I promise, my dear, you'll never be toyed!"

"Join me in laughter, let's play hide and seek,
I'm everywhere and nowhere, so unique!
In the absence of answers, let's make a dance,
Life's a cosmic joke, so take a chance!"

Black holes chuckled, swirling with ease,
While quasars popped popcorn, if you please.
"Life's about giggles, not serious things,
We float through the cosmos like silly kings!"

So I embraced all the empty spaces,
Found joy in odd, and made funny faces.
In the vastness of nothing, I learned to sing,
Life's not a puzzle, it's a cosmic fling!

Chronicles of Cosmic Currents

Across the cosmos, where stars flip and spin,
Came the chronicles of laughter, where giggles begin.
An astronaut told tales of a sun with a frown,
Who turned upside down to avoid wearing a crown!

With planets as potlucks, each brought their dish,
Uranus served beans with a very odd wish.
Jupiter boasted of storms so grand,
While Earth just smiled, "Look at my land!"

Wormholes winked and danced along,
Chasing comets singin' their silly song.
"Why so serious?" a neutron quipped,
"Life's just a ride, so get your grip!"

So gather your friends from galaxies far,
Raise a toast to the cosmos, our bright shining star!
In the chronicles of laughter, we find our way,
With smiles orbiting, come what may!

Threads of Destiny in Nebulae

In cosmic threads we tango and twirl,
Stars giggle and laugh, life's a swirl.
A comet slips, and oh, what a mess,
Is it fate or just a cosmic guess?

Planets gossip in orbits wide,
As black holes munch on space-time's pride.
We dance on quarks, a disco ball,
Who knew the void had such a call?

Asteroids hum a rock 'n' roll beat,
Galaxies wink and can't be beat.
With every twinkle, a jest ensues,
In this grand joke, we've paid our dues.

So here we are, on stardust's stage,
Not a script in hand, just a cosmic page.
Life's a laugh, a silly cheer,
In this universe, nothing to fear!

A Journey Through Starlit Realms

Off we go on a spaceship bright,
Chasing dreams in the dead of night.
The Milky Way serves cosmic ice cream,
Each scoop a giggle, a stellar dream.

Wormholes twist, like spaghetti strands,
Time's a noodle in the universe's hands.
We'll put on socks, mismatched for fun,
In starry lands, the jest's just begun.

Black holes burp in a galactic play,
As meteors dance like they're on a stray.
Gravity's pulling, but we'll just float,
With laughter echoing, we'll rock the boat.

So pack a punchline, a joke or two,
In this grand ride, it's all up to you.
With stars as our guides and humor in tow,
A joyous journey, let's go with the flow!

Beyond the Horizon of Being

Imagine life, a cosmic joke,
Where even stars bend to have a poke.
Beyond horizons, where giggles reign,
Even the void can't contain the gain.

Astrophysics? Just a fancy word,
For laughter echoing, absurdly heard.
Enlightenment hides in quantum quips,
As reality winks and does flips.

Duck and cover from meteoric pies,
In space, no one sees your surprised eyes.
Planets chuckle at our silly plight,
What does it matter? We're shining bright!

So let's embrace this cosmic jest,
With humor etched in every quest.
Life's a riddle in a starlit glow,
In the grand scheme, we'll just go with flow!

Celestial Harmonies in the Void

In the void, where silence laughs,
Echoes of whimsy chart our paths.
Stars strum chords in a playful way,
Singing tunes of a cosmic play.

Meteor showers, like confetti rain,
Life's a dance of joy and strange pain.
The universe tickles at every turn,
In the cosmic kitchen, there's so much to learn.

Life's a puzzle with pieces askew,
A cosmic riddle just for me and you.
So grab a quasar, and pull up a chair,
Let's toast to the chaos, breathing the air!

With harmonies soaring, we beam with glee,
In the vast expanse, we're meant to be free.
In celestial laughter, we find our way,
In this grand void, let's frolic and play!

The Poetry of Quantum Existence

In the dance of a particle's spin,
Where cats both flee and grin,
A universe giggles in strings,
Playing solo in cosmic flings.

Photons race with a wink,
As atoms bob, spiral, and blink,
Life is a game of dice,
Where 'chance' has a plan quite nice.

Every thought's a wave, it seems,
Sailing through the ocean of dreams,
Laughing at logic, what a twist!
In this realm, who could resist?

So sip on stardust, take a ride,
Join the quirks that science hides,
For in this fun of quantum flair,
Existence sparkles everywhere!

A Tapestry Woven in Time

Threads of laughter weave the night,
Stitching moments, oh so bright,
With each tick of the cosmic clock,
We dance to a whimsical rock.

Time wears socks that never match,
Creating memories we can catch,
Oh, what fun this tapestry brings,
Knitting giggles, snorts, and flings!

Past and future play hide and seek,
In this game, we are quite unique,
Caught between a grin and a sigh,
Chasing clouds that float on by.

So grab your yarn and start to weave,
In colors that you can't believe,
As laughter stitches through the seams,
Life's just a patchwork of dreams!

Songs of Stars and Solitudes

Beneath a sky where stars have fun,
They sing and twirl, each one a pun,
Galaxies giggle in shadows that play,
While comets waltz on their cosmic ballet.

Shooting stars make wishes with flair,
As space dust dances in chilled, cool air,
Black holes chuckle, their secrets they keep,
Pulling in thoughts that drift off to sleep.

Constellations chat in twinkling light,
Bantering tales through the velvet night,
Life's a laugh on a stellar stage,
With the universe writing every page.

So join the choir of celestial glee,
In the symphony of infinity,
Where solitude sings and stars align,
Life's a tune you'll find divine!

The Maze of Cosmic Whispers

In a maze where whispers giggle,
And shadows stumble with a wiggle,
The cosmos plays a jolly game,
Where questions are wild but answers tame.

Galaxies prance in spirals vast,
While echoes of laughter roar and blast,
"Where do we go?" a sly voice asks,
"Just follow the stars, and don't drop your tasks!"

Each corner turns with a silly twist,
Inflated egos are often missed,
Quantum paths lead the curious ones,
To ponder life's riddle with more fun runs.

So take a step, beware the glee,
In this cosmic maze, just let it be,
For whispers are secrets we hold tight,
While laughter spins our cosmic night!

Whispers of Cosmic Truth

In the void, stars giggle bright,
Planets waltz in silly light.
Galaxies swirl in a cosmic spree,
Do they ponder 'Why are we?'

Comets race with tails like kites,
Asteroids throw cosmic bites.
Black holes gulp with a grand cheer,
'It's all a joke, my dear!'

Nebulas paint with colors wide,
While quarks play hide and seek inside.
Life's just a joke on a grand scale,
Even atoms laugh without fail!

So when you ponder truth divine,
Remember, the stars sip on wine.
In this cosmic circus, we're all jesters,
Life's a comedy, full of testers.

Starlit Reflections on Existence

In the dark, the planets grin,
Hula hoops of Saturn spin.
Jupiter winks with a gas-giant flair,
While Mars laughs, saying, 'Life's rare!'

The Milky Way spills cosmic milk,
As stardust dances, oh-so-silk.
Stars collide in a glittery clash,
'Oops!' they chuckle, 'What a bash!'

Light years stretch between their jest,
In the cosmos, can we find rest?
Yet here we sit, on a spinning rock,
Wondering 'who's there to unlock?'

Eons pass in a cosmic reel,
Our existence? It's all surreal.
Laugh with the stars, take a leap,
In this universe, secrets we keep.

Dancing Among the Celestial Threads

Cosmic threads weave tales of fun,
While stars play tag in the evening sun.
A quasar jokes, 'Here comes the light,'
As supernovae burst, what a sight!

Galaxies spin in a lovely dance,
Planets trip, in a solar romance.
In this vast dance hall, everyone prances,
Winking at fate, taking their chances.

Asteroids bob to a silent tune,
While aliens giggle at the shape of the moon.
Life flips and flops in this cosmic ballet,
Each twist and turn, a marvelous sway.

So grab a partner, float with glee,
In this universe, wild and free.
With a wink and a nod, we twirl and spin,
Among the stars, let laughter begin!

Echoes from the Infinite

In the vastness where echoes roam,
Black holes whisper, 'Welcome home!'
Stars chuckle, twinkling bright,
'We're just playing hide and seek tonight!'

Galactic wonders, comical schemes,
Nebulas float like whimsical dreams.
'Are we real?' asks a passing quark,
'Just check the jokes from the cosmic park!'

Life's a riddle wrapped in a smile,
Wormholes guide us, mile by mile.
In this universe, bizarre and grand,
Laughter sprinkles like stardust sand.

So pay heed to the cosmic jest,
Every moment's a chance to rest.
Embrace the giggles, take a chance,
In this stellar ballet, let's all dance!

A Pilgrim Among the Stars

I packed my snacks and set my sights,
On cosmic pies and meteor bites.
With aliens waving their greenish arms,
I thought I'd find universal charms.

They showed me the taffy clouds up high,
And we giggled as comet tails flew by.
Yet every deep thought was met with a grin,
As they said, 'You'll find wisdom in jellybean skin!'

In black hole cafes, I sipped cosmic foam,
While discussing if wormholes could lead you home.
Yet when I asked, 'What's life all about?'
They laughed so hard, I had to doubt.

So here I roam, a traveler bold,
Searching for meaning in starlight so cold.
I might find clarity, or just a good laugh,
As I tumble through space on this candy-filled path.

Visions in the Celestial Expanse

Up there are giants, they roll and they play,
Doing cartwheels on Saturn's rings all day.
I asked them their secrets to life under stars,
They handed me snacks from interstellar bars.

With creatures of hue that put rainbows to shame,
Each told me a different philosophical game.
One claimed to find wisdom in a donut's hole,
While another swore it was love for a whole.

In this vast expanse where silly meets wise,
The truth seemed to vanish in bursts of surprise.
With each cosmic giggle, the universe smiled,
Like a ticklish child, forever beguiled.

So I dance with the stars and sprinkle the dust,
For laughter, they say, is the universe's must.
If fun is the answer, then I'll take the leap,
And find my delight in dreams that we keep.

From Stardust to Sentience

Once a speck of dust in a swirling storm,
I woke to the thought, 'What's the cosmic norm?'
The stars winked down and gave me a nudge,
As I pondered if life was just a big fudge.

Galaxies giggled like children at play,
While I searched for wisdom in their sparkly sway.
They chirped, 'Don't be solemn, just start to prance!
Life's just a chance for a silly dance!'

From quarks to quirks, the tale unwinds,
The universe chuckles as it rewinds.
With each rotation, new comedies bloom,
And I laugh at the chaos, embracing the room.

With each cosmic turn, new giggles arise,
The answer, I guess, is in joy-filled skies.
As I float through this life, a stardust delight,
I'll keep laughing on through the deep, endless night.

Celestial Echoes of Our Being

In a void where echoes of laughter stay,
The universe hums a curious play.
Stars moan with joy in a comedic tune,
As planets joke around the pockmarked moon.

I asked a comet, 'What's your plan for today?'
It replied, 'Just zoom and then frolic away!'
While black holes whispered, 'We're never on time,
But catch us in chaos, we'll give you a rhyme!'

With each playful twirl and dancing delight,
The cosmos keeps spinning, both day and night.
In this grand comedy of infinite lore,
I find every ending opens new doors.

So I'll bob with the moons and swing with the stars,
Casting off worries like old, rusted cars.
In the vast cosmic joke, may I always find glee,
For laughter's the key to what's meant to be free.

The Unwritten Code of Existence

In the grand scheme, we're all a joke,
Stars chuckle softly, in cosmic smoke.
Planets dance in their dizzying waltz,
While black holes munch on our tiny faults.

Galaxies swirl like a celestial feast,
Life's a riddle; we're the punchline at least.
Time ticks on like a playful prank,
As comets whiz by, laughing, 'What's your rank?'

We're dust on a whim, a quirk in the void,
Even the universe is sometimes annoyed.
So we stumble and bumble in this cosmic game,
Playing hide and seek with a godly name.

So when you ponder, just keep it light,
Even stars giggle in the black of night.
For in this chaotic, hilarious ride,
The secret may just be a cosmic slide!

Celestial Questions in a Sea of Stars

Why do we exist? A cosmic jest,
Stars twinkle down like a stand-up fest.
Galaxies giggle at our tiny dreams,
As we chase shadows and float on beams.

Jupiter's frowning, but don't take it hard,
Even the big guys find life quite marred.
Saturn rings in with a quip or two,
As if to say, 'What's wrong with you?'

Nebulae fluff their colorful hair,
While supernovae shout, 'Life's not fair!'
Yet in this cosmic circus, we dance along,
With stars as our band, we'll sing a funny song.

So chuckle with comets, waltz with the moon,
In this vast universe, you're the right tune.
When questions rise, just laugh out loud,
For we're part of this cosmic, wacky crowd!

Harmonies of Light and Shadow

In shadows cast by lunar beams,
We find our place amid cosmic themes.
Life's a duet of giggles and sighs,
Where even the void sometimes replies.

Planets harmonize in a cheeky song,
As humor whispers, 'You just can't go wrong!'
A wink from Mercury, a grin from Mars,
Reminds us of laughter among the stars.

Celestial tunes bring joy to our plight,
As black holes play games in the midst of night.
We dance with our quirks in a stellar ballet,
The universe chuckles, 'What else can we say?'

So sway with the cosmos, let worries take flight,
For life is a jest in the endless starlight.
Embrace the silly, enjoy the parade,
In this quirky existence, our joy won't fade!

The Poetry of Stardust Dreams

In dreams made of stardust, we laugh and we play,
With cosmic drifters in a whimsical sway.
Life's just a giggle wrapped in a verse,
Where humor and mystery endlessly disperse.

Each twinkle a chuckle, each spiral a jest,
Even the universe puts laughter to the test.
While meteors race like they're late for a show,
We crash through the cosmos with a giggly glow.

Quasars sizzle with stories untold,
As we sip cosmic tea, sharing jokes old.
The sun tickles Earth, making flowers bloom bright,
As the moon winks gently, saying, 'Not quite night.'

So in this grand poetry, let humor beam,
For life's just a dance on a starlit dream.
Embrace every quirk, let laughter prevail,
In this cosmic adventure, let joy set the sail!

Navigating the Cosmos of Thought

In the vast expanse of a thought,
Ideas float like cosmic dust.
Stars blink with witty replies,
While black holes munch on our trust.

Asteroids swirl in a dance,
Believing they know what to do.
Meanwhile, comets arm-wrestle,
Claiming they're older than you!

Planets giggle in their orbits,
Joking with moons, what a sight!
Gravity pulls them together,
But they still love to take flight.

Each thought is a journey we take,
With laughter echoing through space.
So, buckle up, it's a wild ride,
In this cosmic, humorous race!

Journeys through Celestial Shadows

In shadows cast by starlit glee,
The universe whispers its plans.
Planets play hide-and-seek,
While galaxies giggle in pans.

Stars throw shade on your worries,
Claiming that's all part of the game.
While comets are trading old tales,
Razzing one another with names.

Nebulas puff up with pride,
Each one a cosmic surprise.
"Look at my color!" they boast,
As supernovae wink with their eyes.

We stumble through stardust so bright,
Finding meaning in faraway jest.
Each cosmic riddle brings laughter,
In this universe, we are blessed!

Skies of Forgotten Dreams

In skies where dreams dare to float,
Laughter echoes among the stars.
While shooting stars have a blast,
Sharing "Remember when?" memoirs.

Clouds dress like floating marshmallows,
Daring astronauts to munch bold.
Jupiter's storms crack wise,
While wisdom in silence unfolds.

Dare to chase whims of the night,
For starlight dances and sways.
Even black holes have a sense,
Filching jokes from ancient days.

So gather your dreams, don't delay,
In the skies where laughter reigns.
Cosmic giggles beam from afar,
Within the wonder that remains!

The Sweetness of Cosmic Embrace

In the embrace of the moonlit glow,
Stars whisper secrets, oh so sweet.
Galaxies huddle, trading smiles,
While comets do a joyful beat.

Asteroids throw a surprise party,
Bouncing to music from afar.
"Who wants cake?" they call out loudly,
It's always fun, even in a jar!

Stardust sprinkles on wise old suns,
Each grain holds laughter and cheer.
While cosmic winds swirl and twirl,
Lost in the tickles we hear.

So cherish the sweetness of space,
For humor shapes our galactic race.
With every giggle from above,
The universe wraps us in love!

Embracing the Infinite Now

In pajamas of stars we dwell,
Tickling comets, ringing the bell.
Time's a jolly, whimsical jest,
Dance with the quirks, it's for the best.

Galaxies giggle, swirling around,
Laughing at notions of lost and found.
Life's a brief joke, don't take it too hard,
Just keep your heart light, and your mind unbarred.

We chase the light on this spinning sphere,
Sipping on stardust, we have no fear.
Each moment's a gift, so drop the despair,
And ride the waves of the cosmic flair.

So wear your laughter like a fine cloak,
Shuffle your feet, let the stars provoke.
In the jig of the cosmos, we float and spin,
With each twinkling test, just let the fun begin!

Beneath Celestial Canopies

Under the dome of a cosmic show,
We munch on moonbeams, stealing the glow.
Planets spin tales, some silly, some wise,
They giggle and wink with starlit eyes.

Beneath the vast sky, a picnic so bright,
We toast to the quirks of a silly night.
Asteroids dodge in a comedic flight,
Who knew space could be such a delight?

Galactic squirrels hoard little dreams,
Swirling around in their fluffy schemes.
A dance of atoms, a chuckle here,
Life's a big party, pause for a cheer!

With each comet's tail, we throw our cares,
Tracing the giggles woven in prayers.
Beneath the ether, we play and we jest,
In the laughter of stardust, we find our rest.

Dreams Written in Nebulae

In the tapestry of the night sky,
Dreams scribbled in clouds, oh my, oh my!
With sprinkle of giggles and cosmic grace,
Nebulae dance like they're in a race.

Twinkling thoughts in wisps of delight,
Cosmic conundrums, a whimsical sight.
With every star that we see twirl and nod,
We wander the wonders, in laughter we plod.

Silly shadows of quasars leap,
Whispering secrets, and promises keep.
Chasing our wishes on stardust trails,
Seems the universe loves its own tales.

So grab a wish, don't take it too tame,
For in this ballet, there's no one to blame.
When dreams meet the cosmos, oh what a ride,
In this saga of chuckles, let joy be your guide!

Sunswept Revelations

As sunbeams giggle in morning rays,
We bounce through life in whimsical ways.
From solar flares to gentle beams,
Every dawn spins laughter into dreams.

With a wink from the stars, we start our day,
Chasing the sunbeams that lead us to play.
Each flicker of light a jester's cheer,
We wear our grins like candy, never fear.

In the sunshine's glow, we embrace the fun,
Every sidestep in the dance so well spun.
The cosmos chuckles at our little plight,
Reminding us all to savor the light.

So twirl like a planet, in joy and grace,
In this vast universe, find your own place.
For life's but a comedy, and oh what a scene,
With sunswept adventures, let laughter be seen!

Glimpses of Eternity's Heart

In the garden of stars, we giggle and twirl,
Time ticks like a clock in a cosmic swirl.
Planets take selfies, stars throw confetti,
But here on Earth, we're still not quite ready.

Galaxies gossip in a wobbly dance,
Comets are trendsetters, 'Hey, take a chance!'
They laugh at our worries, so small, so absurd,
While we chase our tails, chasing wisdom unheard.

The moon's in a mood, wearing shades of blue,
'What's up with humans? They haven't a clue!'
Maybe we're puzzles, with pieces misplaced,
Or just some lost socks, floating 'round in space.

So let's toast to the stars, let the laughter ignite,
For in this wild universe, we're all just light!
With a wink from a quasar, and a wink from a cat,
We're just cosmic giggles, and how about that?

Resonance of the Galaxy's Breath

In a galaxy far, where the wackiness beams,
Life might just be a series of dreams.
Stars hum a tune, while black holes just yawn,
'Wake us up later—when you're all gone!'

The universe spins, dips, and turns,
While we humans fumble and make our concerns.
Asteroids chuckle, yeah, dust on our hair,
While we seek answers, wondering if they care.

Nebulas burst with colorful glee,
'Look at those Earthlings drinking their tea!'
Maybe they chuckle at our big existential sighs,
Or they write our stories, in the cosmic skies.

Each heartbeat a whisper, each laugh a bright spark,
In this quirky cosmos, we leave our mark.
So let's dance with the moons, and laugh with the sun,
For life's just a comedy, and we're all having fun!

Cosmic Questions of Existence

Why's the sky blue, and cats play with yarn?
What do stars think about before dawn?
The universe's whispers, scattered like dust,
Tell tales of existence, with laughter and trust.

Aliens ponder while sipping green slime,
'Why do humans race against the clock's chime?'
They chuckle in ships that groove and glide,
While we're stuck in traffic, just trying to bide.

Here on the blue planet, we squabble and shout,
Over trivial things, but that's what it's about.
Maybe it's comedy, with punchlines galore,
As we giggle at life, whilst looking for more.

So let's paint the cosmos with humor and cheer,
For in the vastness, friends, we're all crystal clear.
It's a cosmic giggle, a whimsical ride,
In the grand tapestry, we're all intertwined!

Stardust and the Nature of Being

We're all just stardust, a glittery mess,
In a universe busy, trying to impress.
Planets play tag, while black holes consume,
And we humans just worry about our next Zoom.

Atoms are chuckling, they join in the fun,
'Dancing through space, isn't this a run?'
Gravity pulls us, just like our dreams,
While the universe giggles, bursting at the seams.

'Hey! What's the rush?' the comets all shout,
While we lose our socks, in the great cosmic spout.
Maybe the key is just to be free,
And embrace our oddities, as bright as can be.

So let's twirl with the planets, and hop with delight,
In the grand spectacle of day and of night.
For in this weird journey, we're just having a blast,
As we dance through existence, from first breath to last.

www.ingramcontent.com/pod-product-compliance
Lightning Source LLC
Chambersburg PA
CBHW051641160426
43209CB00004B/736